So, I'll stay,

Sitting with You...

A collection of poems and prayers

by Britny Virginia

Graphic cover by

Esther and Emmanuel Phillips

@jungelqueen @verkehrt

@philldrips

Disclaimer: I have made every effort to contact all copyright holders.

Copyright © 2020 Britny Virginia

For inquiries email britnyvirginiaa@gmail.com

Paperback: ISBN

First paperback edition: October 2020.

Edited by Joy Jungle UK
Cover Art by Esther Phillips
Art Refiner by Emmanuel Phillips
Proofreaders by Candice Mante, Simon Trodd and Elsa Gore
Layout by Britny Virginia

Excerpt from "King James Holy Bible" by Bible Gateway.

Public Domain.

Excerpt from "Jesus Loves Me" by Anna Bartlett Warner
Public Domain.

Printed by Printing UK in the UK

Remus House

Coltsfoot Drive

Woodston

Peterborough

PE2 9BF

www.bookprintinguk.com/

Kindle Direct Publishing

kdp.amazon.com/en_US

For more from Britny Virginia visit

www.britnyvirginiaa.com/

Thank you, mom and dad, for always loving me.

Thanks to all those who have supported my writing over the years even when I didn't believe in my own work.

Thank you to my proof-readers: Simon Trodd, Candice Mante, Charlotte Lavender and Elsa Gore.

And thank you to our sweet Nennen for proofreading the St. Lucian Creole for me!

This is for my lonely nights and the God who stays.

Contents

1.<u>YHWH</u>

Da. Dada, I am unfit to love You. Weed out my iniquities and make me whole, Dada. Make me whole. Make me hole, Dada. Holy.

I long to be Holy. But I am just a broken man.

Pa. Papa, my lips are deceitful. My lips have denied you, thrice. When my lips touched Your skin,

Did it sting? It stung me. I was an unappreciative bee to Your garden.

Bo. Bondyé, is what the Lucians call You. I am a piece of clay, surrounded by the sea of You. I've heard You like to use clay To perform miracles.

The potter and His chosen clay.

Pa. Papa mwen. My Papa says, take His hand. He is my lifeboat. Papa said hold on when I slipped.

YHWH is an inscription of love for me. Da. Dada. Forgive me. Dada still loves me. Dada says, 'come home.'

So, I'll Stay, Sitting with You

'Come home,' Dada says.

2. Ready Writer

My tongue is the pen of a ready writer
Way, way, weighty
My tongue is the pen of a weighty writer

Weighed down by uncertainty
Weighed down by insecurity
Way, way, weighty
Life is weighty

My heart is the pen of a heavy writer
Heavily filled with murk

I sometimes cannot think
I sometimes cannot breathe
I sometimes cannot love
Nor can I receive love

My credo teaches me to do in order to receive
But not so according to You

You tell me to receive and do

Receive and do

But I cannot do

That

My woes are mediocre, but my day is consumed with

anxiety and dread

I sometimes dread the day

At times my tongue is the pen of a ready writer

Other times, I cannot lift it to the roof of my mouth to speak

3. In my feelings or in my Truths?

Dusty boots and crooked legs. I've been condemned to such

disillusionment. I am not strong like my mother.

My mother is a tongue I cannot speak.

My mother is a delicacy I cannot swallow, and a reservoir that

flows from an endless stream.

She's been drugged with strength and dignity - strength and dignity.

But I am not so. I've lost my way to Hope.

It's dark and misty in my heart.

Help me, moon! Help me, Son!

Help me overcome the dread that awaits my soul at noonday.

I'm pretty but crippled. Pretty crippled.

The cult of discouragement has lured me into despair.

FALLEN to my knees. I've lost my life in You.

I am a mess- a failure of sorts.

But still, Your heart is kind and Your song rustles

through the anxiety in my breath.

Dusty boots and crooked crosses beheld redeeming blood.

Crooked crosses straighten crooked legs - and crooked hearts.

The crown of thrones has now become my horn.

Hope sprung from the dead and proclaimed,

'He is not here, He has risen!'

Risen! Alas!

I am no longer a prisoner of shame but

now a patriarch for the Gospel.

4. Lost

Father!

    Hold me and never let go.

Father!

    I shout Your name but to no prevail!

Father!

    I am a fading shadow- a passing wind.

DADDY!

    My life is like a shooting star!

    I cannot reach.

FAR!

Your Name is far

From me.

FURTHER away when I say

FAR-THER!

father!

    Help the imbecile within me.

FATHER!

    How do You see me?

Abba?

How do you see me when I've forgotten You?

Abba?

How do you see me when I've forgotten

myself in the depths of my pain?

FATHER!

I'm lost when I say FATHER!

Daddy issues, daddy issues.

DADA. DADA! Abba!

I am a cyclone of failure.

FATHER!

Do you still love me?

FADA! Answer me,

FADA!

FATHER!

FATHER!

Please save me.

FATHER!

Please love me.

Father.

5. I am good at this courage thing

I am not as strong as you'd think

I am not as courageous as you'd deem

I wake up and all I can desire is to be done with the day

Or how the day would be better off without me

I am a pile of broken promises, wishes and dreams

I am the tally mark of unanswered prayers

I am the desert dew if the desert had dew

I am cold and withering away

But there in the wind goes a still small voice that sings

Jesus loves me this I know

I am not as strong as you think I am

I am not as wise as you'd perceive

I am not as courageous as you'd deem

So, why did You call me?

Why did You choose me?

I am a skyscraper about to fall

I am an ill-structured submarine

I am going to sink

I am going to drown

Hitting the ocean floor

Along with Lucy

She disappeared once

But even in the low

There goes Your song

In the haunted gales of my heart

It reaches far and wide

*This thing I **don't** know*

What does it mean to be loved by Jesus?

I'd wonder this in my sleep but never utter these words out loud

They're a secret you see

Because I'm meant to know the answer

I'm meant to be strong

But how I thank God, He breaks forth

And leads me in song

Jesus loves me this I know

And even when I can't believe

And even when I don't know how to receive

He teaches me

That this here is a courageous thing

This here is true strength

Found only in Him

Through Him

That

Little ones to Him belong

They are weak but He is strong

Yes, Jesus loves me

This is true strength as we sing

Yes, Jesus loves me

This is true knowledge as we believe

Yes, Jesus loves me

The Bible tells me so

Why, why my soul are you downcast?

Why so disturbed within me?

Yes, Jesus does love you.

6. <u>Grace and Mercy Found Me</u>

Love is patient

Love is kind

Love is not jealous

It does not boast

Love is not rude

Love is not self-seeking

Love is not easily provoked

It does not keep a record of wrongdoing

Love does not rejoice in injustice but instead rejoices in Truth

Love bears all things, hopes in all things and endures

in all things (regardless of the outcome)

Love NEVER fails

\-   1 Corinthians 13: 4-8

He called my name but didn't know me. He called my name, but I didn't recognise this stranger's voice. He knew my depths but didn't really know my depths because only Elohim knows my depths. The complexities of a broken spirit, You God delight in- to fix and mend what is out of sorts because we are Your children. You called my name, but instead, I hid in shame

Where are you?

You called out to me.

Where are you my child?

Lord don't come near! I am too filthy!

I am filled with filth! Don't come near to me! I walk further and further away from Your presence, but Your Word says where can I go from Your presence? If I make my bed in Sheol there You are. How come? How come your presence is so present?

How come your presence is so pleasant?

I quiver at the thought of standing within Your view. Lord don't speak to me, I am unworthy.

"Britny, don't you know My Love for you goes far beyond anything you could do or have done?"

"My Love exceeds the shame you feel.

I have loved you with an everlasting love.

15

Come take My hand, My child, how I have loved you!"

Lord, I hear you coming close and Your footsteps thunder. You say You come in peace but my heart trembles with fear. You say take Your hand but what if I fall back into my sin again?

I hear voices. Mutters of joy as my heart joins my mind on a jolly ride back to my sin; as a dog that returns back to its own vomit. The spirit of lust dances to the melody of my afflictions. She laughs at my foolish attempts to be renewed. I say I am made new by Your Spirit but how can I be a new creation every 30 minutes? My past entices me, Lord. Does your love exceed a heart that fails several times a day?

"Seventy times seven. My love exceeds it. Seventy times seven.

Yes, My Love exceeds the brutality of the cross, the whips, the punches, the spit thrown in My face, the mocking, the rebuke, the suffocation, the tearing of my flesh and ligaments, the betrayal, the shame. My Love exceeds the lust that clutches your heart at night, in the morning, and in the afternoon.

My Love exceeds its hold on you because my Love breaks chains and removes strongholds, soul ties and rejection.

16

Yes, rejection. It's a rotten root that has held your heart in chains for years

But I have come so that you may have life and life more abundantly.

I have come so I may set you free and whom the Son sets free is free indeed!

Don't you know that I have known you?

And, I have loved you.

I have chosen you in all your sin, I have chosen you.

Before sin brewed itself within your heart, your name I have known, and I have loved.

Encourager, is who I call you.

You will be an encourager of the Lord, as I use that very sin to quiet the rebuke because my power is perfected in your weakness"

I am not a God that follows the logic of man, but I am a God that confounds man's logic, so my Glory may be lifted."

Encourager. That's funny, Lord.

But don't you need courage to be an encourager?

And courage is what I lack most

To be an encourager you

17

must be able to speak up
and I choke on my words

Now wait, don't tell me,
come close to You and
You will strengthen me
because what if my
affections are not
towards You. What
happens when I don't
want to spend time in the
secret place. Though I
love you, Lord, I
struggle.

*"My Love will draw you
back*

*You may struggle but My
Love will draw you
closer*

*My love will be the
fishing rod that recuses
your heart when it is
drowning in sin*

My love will save you

*I am the good Shepherd
who rescues His sheep
when they stray away.*

I will keep you.

I will keep you.

*I will reach out My hand
towards you.*

*Don't you know My hand
is not too short to save?*

*I will be your Lord and
your God,*

*I will be your Lord and
your God,*

*I am your Lord and your
God.*

*And you will see that I
have loved you.*

And I have known you.

*And I will keep on loving
you – for My grace is*

sufficient."

7. Pages of a Broken Heart

Read the depths of me as a novel.

Like chapters, You've searched and

Written in the quiet of the dawn.

For I am sure You wrote me.

Because You know my rise and my fall.

Light the candle of me when I've been burned out.

Be The Yang to my yin, the Light to my darkness.

Be the Hope that stirs me on when

My heart has wandered off into the abyss.

Abyss. I am a sheep off to the slaughter.

Slaughter the disgust out of me

because Your rod is precious to me.

Teach me how to breathe again

When my lungs have given way.

Teach me the solace of Your voice

In the chaos of my mind.

I am unfaithful

But

You are

not.

8. Before You

Before You, I smile a smile of gratefulness

Before You, I dance a dance of glory

Before You, I am knitted finely to perfection

Before You, I am vindicated and saved

For You, oh God, are my dearest song

A sincere hooray.

9. He Chooses the Other

She poured alabaster oil on His feet. And wiped His feet with her hair. And washed them with her tears. Great was her love for Him and even more His for her. Great was her revelation of Him and even more His overall vision towards her.

She was despised by society- mocked, ridiculed, an outsider, an adulterer, but no one saw the survivor and the virtue within her. No one saw it.

Yet, He did.

And chose her to proclaim His gospel of grace, peace and love. He wasn't concerned with her past as much as He was excited about the future, He'd give to her. He wasn't concerned with the views and opinions that others had about her but instead delightfully sought to love her fiercely at the cost of being condemned Himself.

The Son of Man often chose the weak; the left; the other of this world to draw others out into His marvellous Light. She poured alabaster oil on His feet, giving Him all that she had and carefully wiped His feet with her hair- casting her crown to exalt His and thoughtfully washed them with her tears, mourning His death and rejoicing in His victory.

How I wish I was her

Humble and devout.

I wish I was her,

Unashamed and secure.

How I wish I was her,

Madly and deeply in love

and desperate

to display the extent of that love

For her King, her Lord and her Friend.

I wish I was her.

10. Construction

Being stretched in angles I hadn't flexed before

Made me uneasy,

He told me to trust Him

But this task demanded a death

Yet, I was not ready to give it away

To give myself away

But, unbeknownst to me,

My life had already been spoken for

I was assigned

I was chosen

The idea of freedom tapped me from the inside

But I hated its feel against my organs

It was scaley

And this was uncharted territory

Tali, Tali

Talitha koum

The word was so hard to word it slit my tongue in two

It struck out to me and pierced my soul

Like the wail of a new born babe on its way home

Into its mother's bosom

An oracle of true allegiance

It called out to me as deep calls deep

And deeply

I sunk into its revelation

Of me

11. A letter to my King

The greatness of Your majesty

Keeps me enthralled for eternity.

Paralysed,

I become

In awe of

You.

I

Cannot think

Of a place better

Than the Eden

Of

You.

Create in me a clean

Heart and renew a right spirit

Within me.

Keep me

At

Your

Feet,

Humble

And

Devout.

Keep me

At

Your throne,

Humble

And devoted,

To

You

And You,

Alone.

12. Who Can Love a Poet Like Me?

Who can love a poet like
me?

I'm happy to receive
there's none but Thee.

Who can dance
unashamed?

And laugh aloud with
me?

I'm grateful to conclude
there's none but Thee.

Who can understand my
ways?

And forgive easily?

I'm happy to declare
there's none but Thee.

Who can accept me
fully?

And journey in life
alongside me?

I've come to decree
there's none but Thee.

Who can win souls
joyously?

All,

For Your Glory?

I've come to understand
there's none but Thee.

Who is worthy of my
entirety?

And climb my walls

With vigour and glee

Just to pull them down

And get a glimpse of
me?

I've come to believe
there's none but Thee

And who can run this
race of sacrifice whilst
supporting me?

I've seen, there's none
but Thee.

If I am to walk into
eternity,

Lone of a lover's hand
intertwined,

Grey hair and faint

May I be eternally
grateful for my joy found
in Thee.

But if You deem it

That a suitor is worthy of
me

May I wait patiently,

For the one who You
have known and taught
of the deepest love to be

Let him bow down and
know that

We are only one through
Thee

And let him love Thee
firstly,

Before me,

In doing so he knows,

He'll get the greatest
version of me.

For I am found in You
and nothing else will
ever do

13. This Demon Called Anxiety

Tell me of this demon

It plagues our land

Tell me of this demon

That's a ferocious liar

Tell me of this demon

It viciously decapitates its victims

Tell me of this demon

It engulfs the hearts of generations

Tell me of this demon

That snatches away hope

Tell me of this demon

It's a disease that spreads like wildfire

Tell me of this demon

That prowls around seeking whom it may devour

Tell me of this demon

That God tramples underfoot!

Tell me of this demon

That must bow down at the Name!

Tell me of this demon

That has no hold on me!

Tell me of this demon

That has no authority

Tell me of this demon

That can only taunt me

Tell me of Him and His sovereignty

Whom shall I fear?

Certainly, not this demon

Called anxiety!

14. Known

I have engraved your name at the centre of My palm.

As an architect

establishes their structure, so have I established you

firmly rooted by rivers of living water.

An oak of my righteousness.

I have given you a new name– Obed.

Obed is who I call you—a worshipper and servant for the Lord.

You are evidence of my fingerprint. You are my beloved,

I have set you upon a rock which cannot be removed.

And I have directed your every step.

You belong to Me,

Britny.

You belong to Me.

You are Mine.

15. The Good Shepherd

By day, the Lord directs His love

At night, His song is with me

He's with me

Always and forever

He'll be with me

A prayer to the ages

for my Lord and my God

16. <u>Seasonal</u>

Cruising through Your love has me hooked

On Your rod of grace,

As the tide rhythms away

I won't be put to shame

Because You've got me.

17. In a Distant Land

In a distant land, I will remember You.

Before the day breaks and the early bird captures the worm,

You will be my source,

My rest.

I will lift my head to the heavens;

Where does my help come from?

It comes from the Maker of heaven and earth!

I'm safe inside the grip of Your wing

You'll never leave me

You'll never forsake me

This I know that

In a distant land, You are near.

18. A Superb Truth

Where I once found lack,

You made abundant.

Where I once cried,

You used it to water a harvest.

When I was denied,

You took me through acceptance.

How could I repay such deeds of gold?

It transcends the treasures of this world.

My voice was nay,

It wasn't strong.

But my God, when You stepped in

I was boosted to belong.

When my plate was without,

You filled it with much

You took nothing

And created substance

In just one touch

A nobody was I

But now moulded into

A King

A Queen

A Daughter

And a Son.

You placed embroidered robes on me

And declared me precious.

No longer am I a wasteland,

Rather, the flow of the Euphrates.

19. A Delicate Wonder

Oh death

Oh death

Where is your sting?

Oh, grave

Oh, grave

Where is thy victory?

He's spoken to me of lilies,

How they clothe the field,

But to Him, I am much better

Than all of these.

I still trust in Him,

because He trusts in me

To carry His nature

And to attain my highest degree

He dresses me in clovers

But it's not luck, you see,

It's faith, it's faith

That allows me

To tread

On mountainous trees.

20. <u>Your Faithfulness</u>

This morning was hard

My eyelids were heavy

My heart was cold

This morning I was angry

I was frustrated

I wanted to give up

This morning I wanted revenge

I wanted to lock my heart away

But still, this morning, I felt You,

Sweeping through the graveyard bones that was me

Leading me to a place where peace and joy

was founded on forgiveness

But this morning I wanted to fight against You

and the sweetest in Your holy tug

Still, this morning You won against my every rebuttal

And You led me

And if tomorrow it comes again

The hurt, the pain,

I will remember this morning

And

Your faithful hand.

21. Questions

Why do they all leave, Father?

Am I so hard to love?

Am I so hard to want?

22. A Divine Remedy

What can I compare to Your goodness?

If I were to search,

I would come back empty.

Wine tastes better aged.

That is why I love Your archaic ways,

Oh, Ancient of days.

I'm curious about You.

I am a foreigner of Your love.

Yet, You are my restful haven.

Peel back the walls I've built up

Like brown pepper

But Your eyes don't water.

Because You've known me...

And when my heart failed me

You caught it

To my delight/ surprise.

23. Falling for You

I want to embark on the journey of you.

And sip tea as posh folks do.

I want to travel through the maze of You.

And test the waters as the experts suggest we ought to.

I want to trail through the history of you

And appreciate the tongue your mother spoke when

Whips lashed her skin to sorrow.

I want to love You ever so deeply.

And continue to learn You.

Then relearn what I've unlearned about You.

Because I've come to know there's always more to You

I want to need You.

I want to want You.

Because I've seen that life is a worthless shrine without You.

24. <u>Your Jubilee</u>

Erect in me the jubilee

That waits me ahead.

Subdue these lowly thoughts

That consumes this fragile heart

Console the whimpers that

echo in the night.

Make your home within me

And may I find life in death

and death in life;

As my mourning grows to songs

of praises as a fragrant offering.

25. <u>When We're in the Valley</u>

In the night,

In the night,

You give us songs.

In the night,

In the night,

You become our song.

Our righteous melody...

26. <u>Once more</u>

My heart

is a deep

well

within me...

...Only You

can c

27. For All Eternity

In the house of the Lord, I long to dwell beneath the bough of the crackling oak tree.

Where splinters pierced His open wounds and the sun's rays seep through its leaves. My stomach growls anticipating the great feast. As we sit near riverbanks watching streams flow that quench the thirst of the doe.

Beneath the bough of the Lord's oak tree is heaven's remedy. Branches clap in zealous wonder at the upcoming festivities. Birds chirp and dragonflies' fly. The field is filled with serenity and lilies. Ants march to their tower building. As I trail through the beast's coat. His name captures me like a spark in a forest fire. The sum of praises welcomes the Prince in.

'All Hail the King, the Lamb, the Chosen! None can compare to Thee!'

My heart is safely kept at the hem of His.

Dear God! Dear me! I'm betrothed to His Majesty! Eternally found in His decree, His pleasure, and seal. Locked forever within His promises for me!

Under the sheltering of the old oak tree is where I long to be. In sight of squirrels and rabbits playing.

I'll run along circling the torso of the old tree. Laughing, saying, You can't find me. But You've already sought me. And know the deepest parts I've held. You know my sitting and my standing. My going out and my coming in. You are the great Lion enthroned for eternity!

Day in, day out beneath the old oak tree. The children giggle, whistle and run. Cherubim sings, 'Prepare the way of the Lord!' The elders proclaim His sovereignty. Dressed in robes of white, He welcomes me to join in song of His eternal glory. All of this is mine, He says to me, as He takes my hand to wed me. I'm forever kept safe and belong beneath the Lord's old oak tree.

28. Disability is...

At times

     disability is a noose around my neck,

     As

     I

       hang

    from

       the

Tree of

     Life.

I try to find life as I

     Tip-

     toe

     on the

     rock

     that is

     HIGHER than

     I.

'Fix your eyes on Jesus, Britny!' I hear them shout

But disability is dis-TRACT-ion and FOCUS.

Disability is fighting

and fighting

and fighting

again, to win

only to be

trampled on

again

and losing.

Disability is soaring on the wings of eagles

when I can't stand

I faint under

the

weight

of

disability.

Disability is a mental torment each morning-

It's like s c r e w i n g and *u n s c r e w i n g* a broken appliance again and again.

Disability is break-
    ing
and
rebuild-ing;
     a tearing down
     and restoration.

     Disability is leaving the house
     and forgettin' to love myself
     in my greatest capabilities.

Disability is an olive branch
being birthed
from my chest
only to
bud
into an
orchard

Disability is seeing the sun at night.

Disability is an oxymoron, a paradox

A temperamental matter.

Disability is stiffness and rust

Disability is stretching and ploughing
Disability is
                smiling
                    through
                        the
                            t

                            e

                                        a

                    r

                                                    s.
                Disability is havin' to write this poem on disability.

        Disability is strength and survival.

Disability is the complete and utter surrender that it's not my will but Yours be done.

Disability is **not** knowing

But being certain

That He

Who lives inside of me

Is much greater than

disability.

And if this poem got you tired, I'm glad. Because this is

just one glimpse

Of disability.

29. Jèzi Kwi

Jèzi bon, ich mwen

Ich mwen, Jèzi bon

Jèzi bon tout lé

Maiwé, Jezi Kwi bon tout lé!!

Laviktwa pou Jèzi

Laviktwa pou Jèzi

Ich mwen, mwen asiwé laviktwa pou Jèzi!

Jesus, You have won the victory

The victory belongs to Jesus!

The victory belongs to Jèzi

Jèzi Kwi bon ich mwen!!

Tjenbè, ti fi mwen, tjenbè!

Lavi wèd, ich mwen

Mè ou ni pou tjenbè ti fi!

Ou ni pou tjenbè!

Britny, Jèzi bon tout lè

Tout lè Jèzi bon, ich mwen

Bondyè bon

Tout lè Bondyè bon!

Bondyè bon ich mwen

Mwen asi wé Bondyé bon!!

Tout bagay ni pou twavay, ich mwen

Paski Jézi Kwi bon tout lè

Èpi tout le Jezi bon!

Translation on page 64

30. I will not be subdued

Pouki wèzoni `y tjbene` mwen kon sa, Papa?

Pouki wèzon `y tjbenè mwen kon sa?

Mwen bizwen Ou, Papa mwen!

Mwen bizwen Ou, Senyè!

Mwen bizwen Jehovah Nissi!

Adonai, mwen bizwen!

I really need You, Papa

It holds me down and

Suffocates the promise

Twists it claws deep within and snatches out my intestines

Solely for its pleasure

Mwen bizwen Ou, Papa mwen!

Si se pa t pou Ou Papa, mwen ja mò!

Surely, I would have died without You, Papa!

Mwen taja mò, si se pa t pou Ou!

So, keep me close, Papa mwen

Tjbené mwen

Hold me close to You and never let me go

Èpi lè demou vini mwen pa kai aksèpté.

Translation on page 66

31. Sitting with You

I have always been obsessed with the stride of a woman. Because I always wanted that same stride; beautiful from the ankle up - just like the introduction to the female lead in a black and white film. Or even a coloured movie. I always thought my name sounded better if I were white, ~~BRITTANY~~? Britny. ~~WHITNEY~~? Brit-ny. ~~VERONICA~~? Or I thought if my eyes made a nice curve in the corners and my hair was jet jet black with thick enough lips, I'd be accepted by society; by boys maybe; or perhaps really accepted by myself. But You call me beautiful regardless. You've made me fierce in my infirmity- my flaw, flaw, FLOW! Sitting with You is like the time I floated in the ocean for the first time. Flowing with the waves, my body went up and down. I actually felt safe when I finally let go and allowed the ocean to be. It's being still when I'm sitting with You. Sitting with You is like the warm taste of hot cocoa running down my trachea at nightfall; by the fireplace, if I had one. And if I did like hot cocoa, I don't very much. It sounds nice like I should like it or something, but chocolate in liquid form and hot is confusing to me, just like Your unfailing love. So, tell me, what possesses Someone to die for a stranger? People think I'm crazy or even stupid for believing such tales, but You've called me to be foolish to the wise, for

61

wisdom is subject to foolish ways misunderstood, just like the intellect of my professor. I always hated school. The lessons taught were vague to me. And I wasn't like the other girl over there who always had the right things to say. She even walked so beautifully. Regardless, sitting with You is like Remembrance Day. Dramatic and sorrowful. Grateful and subtle. Puzzling and audacious. Sitting with You is being simply me. It's being read by You and read into you when I'm alone sitting with You. Now tell me, what drives a person to lay down His life for a stranger?

It's so I could be here - sitting with you.

33. <u>Home</u>

Your lips spoke secrets to me.

And I love the privilege of unravelling your mystery. At night your voice was sweet.

It calmed my nerves. Gently I'd cup your face into my palm.

And trace the curve and dance that shapes your smile with my thumb.

I loved catching the gleam in your eye when something excited you.

It sparkled and outshone the multitude of the stars.

I've found the stillness in the hustle and bustle when I am alone with you.

Discovering the depths of your being and flipping through the pages of your heart is my guiltiest pleasure.

I could spend hours immersed in you and still be awed by your perfection.

When my rainbow is aloof Your Son's rain is hopeful.

I'm lost without Your love. I'm lost without Your song in my heart.

I'm lost without the cheer of Your person.

Brings me home.

You, bring me home.

Translations-

Poem 28- Jesus

Jesus is good

        Jesus is good, my child

     My child, Jesus is good all the time

              Of course!

           Jesus Christ is good all the time!!

The victory belongs to Jesus

       The victory belongs to Jesus

         My child, I am sure the victory belongs to Jesus!

Jesus, You have won the victory

       The victory belongs to Jesus!

        The victory belongs to Jesus!

           Jesus Christ is good, my child!!

Hold on my girl, hold on!

        Life is hard

       Life is hard, my child

          But you have to hold on, girl!

           You have to hold on!

Britny, Jesus is good all the time

    All the time Jesus is good, my child

    God is good

    All the time God is good!

God is good, my child

    I am certain, God is good!!

Everything will work out, My child

Because Jesus Christ is good

    All the time!

29. I Will Not Be Subdued

Why is it holding me like that, Father?

Why is it holding me like that?

I need You, my Father!

I need You, my Lord!

I need You Jehovah Nissi!

Adonai, I need You!

I really need You, Papai

It holds me down and

Suffocates the promise

Twists it claws deep within and snatches out my intestines

Solely for its pleasure

I need You, my Father!

If it had not been for You Father, I would have already died!

Surely, I would have died without You, Papa!

I would have already died if it had not been for You!

So, keep me close, my Father

Hold me

Hold me close to You and never let me go

And when the evil one comes, I will not be subdued.

Reference Page

Talitha Koum- Aramaic for 'Little girl, arise!' Found in Mark 5:41.